Project Management

"If you can get experienced project managers to let their guard down for a few moments, they'll probably admit that their first few projects didn't go very well. Be prepared for a rough start as you begin to manage projects. But if you hang in there, you'll find yourself moving up the learning curve rapidly."

"Studies often point to interpersonal and behavioral problems as root causes of project failure. The art of project management is all about getting work done through other people."

"Identifying the customer's true need—the most fundamental problem or opportunity—is the most important step in the entire process."

Project Management

✔ 24 Lessons to Help You Master Any Project

GARY R. HEERKENS

MCGRAW-HILL
New York Chicago San Francisco Lisbon
London Madrid Mexico City Milan New Delhi
San Juan Seoul Singapore Sydney Toronto

1 2 3 4 5 6 7 8 9 0 DOC/DOC 0 9 8 7

ISBN-13: 978-0-07-148652-1
ISBN-10: 0-07-148652-6

Contents

Project Management

☑ The science and art of project management

Project management has a lot of upside potential. First, when done well, it produces positive change that helps you as an individual and your company as a whole. It can also often be a steppingstone to promotion. And it provides a stronger sense of accomplishment and more variety than daily work tasks that never seem to have closure. It often gives people more freedom than they normally enjoy to try new things and take on new tasks and a chance to test and stretch their skills.

Counterbalancing these positives are the challenges that face all project managers. They have to become politically savvy. They have to tolerate more uncertainty and ambiguity than would be acceptable in other areas of work. They have to deal with frustration, especially if they're project managers with responsibility but no authority. The risks are big: having a project go sour can hurt a career far longer than failing in something far less visible.

Project management is both a science and an art.

The science side is learning how to define, coordinate, and document the work. You have to be comfortable working with budgets, estimating time, and deciding what resources are needed. You have to learn how to dig for the true need, not a superficial solution that someone wants to put into place. You have to become comfortable with the tools of project planning: Gantt charts, network diagrams, control plans, and economic value analysis.

The art side is developing your judgment and learning how to lead people. You have to learn to pay attention to details but not get wrapped up in them. You have to make countless decisions with insufficient information and despite conflicting signals. You have to condition yourself to seek acceptable solutions rather than perfect ones. Most project managers work in complex organizations, with team members drawn from several work groups. That creates unique management challenges and puts a high premium on your ability to cultivate a smooth working relationship with many other people inside (and perhaps outside) your organization.

This book covers some of the essentials of the art and science of project management. It talks about defining true needs, building a solid team, and performing a financial analysis. It addresses how you can find the right balance points between extremes like "managing everything vs. managing nothing" and "doing work yourself vs. letting the team do everything." Reading this book will help develop the foundation you need to become a high-performing project manager.

"Although you won't see it addressed in project management reference books, the reality is that mental preparedness may prove to be just as critical to your ultimate success as a project manager as your knowledge base or skill set. Gaining a sound understanding of what's involved in this new role is a critical step toward being mentally prepared."

□ Feel your way around

☑ Understand the PM's role

In some ways, leading a project is much like leading a department: You need to coordinate the efforts of people with diverse backgrounds and skills in hopes of getting the best overall result. But in other ways, leading a project is very different. For one thing, the people you're bringing together may not know each other. Second, a project by definition is unique; it has never been done before. The end product and the process for producing it cannot be fully specified in advance; otherwise, you'll be closed to new learning and opportunities. Third, unlike a department head, a project leader may have no direct authority or control over the members of the team.

So you may find yourself in a position without formal authority, working with people who have never worked together before, and facing a high degree of uncertainty—but, like any other manager, accountable for achieving business goals. Your choices are to waste time feeling your way through each project or to build your understanding of project management skills so your teams can quickly become productive.

To some extent, project success will depend on personality traits like honesty, tolerance for ambiguity, and openness. But equally important are the skills required to make a process go smoothly: paying constant attention to communication (making sure that you, the project sponsors, and the team members are clear on boundaries and expectations), documenting the project process (tasks, responsibilities, relationships), and understanding customer and business needs.

To boost your ability to effectively lead a project:

Develop process management skills: Learn tools for coordinating the work of many people. Get comfortable dealing with managers on issues of expectations, cost, schedule, and resources.

Build your interpersonal skills: Project management is all about getting things done *through other people*. Work on written and oral communication skills. Learn how to negotiate and influence. Become a coach and mentor to your project members.

Build a support network: In all likelihood, your project will involve issues that are beyond your own area of expertise. You should educate yourself as much as possible about the work your organization does, but it also helps to make contacts with people from diverse areas of your company—finance, IT, marketing, technical experts.

"Avoid the trap of believing that because you've been put 'in charge' of a project, you've risen above your peers and that friendships no longer matter . . . The interpersonal and behavioral aspects of project life are crucial to success."

☐ ~~Do it all yourself~~

☑ Build a solid team

Because project managers are under a lot of pressure to perform, they are often tempted to do the project work themselves, especially when team members are floundering. You must learn to avoid this temptation for two reasons. First, you don't and can't know everything. Teams are formed because your company believes that achieving a particular goal or solving a problem can best be done by bringing together people with different perspectives. Second, people come onto a team with the expectation that they are there for a reason, that their knowledge, experience or skills can help the team succeed. If denied a chance to contribute, they will feel cheated.

Finding the right balance between letting people grow their own skills and stepping in to avoid disastrous delays or wrong pathways is one of the hardest things that project managers have to do. You can get off on the right foot by letting people

develop a sense of ownership from the very beginning. Have your team members participate in helping to shape the project scope and definition (in
negotiation with the sponsor, of course).

As the project progresses, share as much decision making as possible. Let the *team* decide when
to meet, develop a plan for rotating meeting responsibilities, develop ground rules for participation,
and assign project responsibilities. Let the team
decide how to make decisions—when consensus is
required, when to defer to someone with expert
knowledge, etc. You are there to make sure nothing
is missed and provide guidance when needed.

Fostering motivation is not difficult to do if you:

Demonstrate that people matter: Explain to team
members their responsibilities and how each person's work contributes to the team's success.
Acknowledge contributions that might normally go
unnoticed.

Convey confidence in your team: Avoid the temptation to micro-manage. Letting people "muddle
through" sometimes gives them confidence they can
figure things out on their own. Assign stretch goals.
Move decision-making authority as close to the
frontline as possible.

Recognize good performance: Set a high standard
for performance. In team meetings and in any team
documentation (notes, bulletin boards, etc.), make

sure the names of contributing team members are featured prominently. Point out good performances to the team sponsor/manager.

"It's not a good idea for you to define and plan the project work alone, then simply hand it to team members to implement. They'll feel that they're executing your plan, not theirs, and performance is likely to suffer."

☑️ Understand the true need

At the beginning of a project, it's natural to have a picture in your head about how everything will unfold. Then reality sets in. Unanticipated problems and opportunities arise. Data show that customer needs are different than what everyone thought. Your choice: continue with the original plan or change the plan based on lessons learned. Successful organizations favor the latter. They recognize that exposing and solving the *true need*—the most basic problem—will pay greater returns in the long run.

Identifying the true need can be tricky. For one thing, many times a project is defined as a *solution* rather than a *need to be fulfilled*. "Install a new production line," for example, is a solution for the true need of "meet customer delivery requirements." Effective project managers always delve for the true needs because they may find alternative ways of meeting that need that are faster, cheaper, more efficient, etc., than the original solution. What company wouldn't be happy if a team could double on-time delivery *without* installing a new production line?

If presented with a project that is really *solution jumping*, try asking a number of people one simple question: "Why?" Probe. Why is the project described this way? What is the problem that people are trying to solve? Where is performance falling short of the goals?

Be forewarned that sometimes this probing can be risky, especially in organizations where data does not yet rule. The manager sponsoring the project may wonder if you're questioning his or her judgment. People may think you're procrastinating.

To probe for a true need without treading on toes:

Document the problem or opportunity: Describe the gap between current performance levels and where you need to be. List the effect of this gap, including the impact on people inside and outside your company. Describe the risks of ignoring this gap and the benefits of closing it.

Share the document: Use the documentation as the basis for a discussion with the functional manager sponsoring the project. Present it as your interpretation of the current state and ask for input and clarification.

Get approval to focus on the true need: If you proceed without approval, your performance may suffer because you did not achieve the original project goal.

"You cannot be certain that you'll satisfy the true need unless you know what it is."

☑ Perform a financial analysis

There is not a company in the world that can afford to waste money on projects that generate insufficient return. Increasingly, a key role played by project managers is tracking the financial investment and return on their projects.

Four common metrics are net present value, internal rate of return, payback period, and cash hole. Net present value (NPV) answers the question, "How much money will this project make or save?" NPV estimates the *present* value of all current and future cash flows resulting from the project. In other words, what are the *long-term results* from this project worth *today*?" Internal rate of return (IRR) projects how rapidly an investment will be returned. Payback period estimates how long it will take to reach a breakeven point. Cash hole (also known as the *maximum exposure*) is an estimate of the largest amount of money invested at any point in time.

These metrics are all part of a complete financial analysis. Estimates done *before* a project are essential for helping your management decide which projects are worthy of investment and how that investment will affect your company's finances in both the short term and the long term. The assessment will be valid only if the analysis includes all the ways in which a project will affect revenue, growth, and expenses. The figures should be updated during and after a project as your knowledge improves about what it will take to achieve the financial goals.

Participate in the financial analysis by helping to:

Estimate cash inflows: Think broadly to identify all the ways in which your project may help increase dollars taken in or the portion of those dollars your company can keep. Consider increased revenue from higher sales, greater margins due to lower operating costs, material savings, and waste reduction.

Estimate cash outflows: Identify any expenditures incurred for the project, including salaries, material, equipment, IT, external consultants, etc. Think too about ongoing expenses that may result, such as increased operating costs.

Construct a cash flow table: Summarize outflows and inflows by year (or by quarter, depending on your industry). Work with internal financial experts to identify the discounted value if your project results will accumulate over years, to account for inflation.

"Although you may not be intimately involved in completing a full financial analysis, as a project manager, you should understand how it's done and the terminology involved."

☐ Just get going

☑ Conduct a formal kickoff

With the increasing pace of business, there is a tendency to favor a "Just go do it!" mentality and underplay the significance of ceremony. That attitude can work to the detriment of project success, because taking the time to plan and conduct a formal kickoff meeting, involving both team members and the sponsoring manager(s), helps in a number of ways.

First, it signals to the entire company that this project is something supported by management and therefore worthy of support from others. Second, it provides a chance for the team to review (or develop) the project charter. Having a common understanding of purpose is critical to being an effective team. Third, it gives the team a chance to interact with management and establish rapport that may help later in the project. Fourth, it gives team members a chance to decide how they want to conduct the team's business. Last but not least, it gives team members a chance to get to know each other personally in a low-pressure situation.

In short, a good kickoff meeting will help make sure that everyone is starting on the same page and headed in the same direction. Failure to understand management expectations has historically been one of the biggest contributors to failed projects. In contrast, giving the team members time to establish relationships among themselves and with management will pay big dividends down the road when the team goes through difficult times (which all teams do).

To have a successful kickoff meeting you should:

Identify which stakeholders should attend: Minimally, you want all team members present and the manager(s) with ultimate accountability for the results. Depending on the project, you may also want to invite staff from the work areas likely to be affected by the project (to help set their expectations and get their buy-in) and/or representative customers whose needs you are addressing.

Plan for management presentations: Sure, you could simply pass along what you know about management's requirements to your team members. But nothing will emphasize the need for, importance of, and commitment to a project quite like hearing it from a manager.

Use time effectively: This first meeting will set the tone for all future team meetings. Employ team meeting tools—agendas, flip charts, discussion methods, etc.—to make sure the time is used well.

"Kickoff meetings can energize a team . . . and rapidly promote team cohesion."

☐ ~~Stick to original vision~~

☑ Pause for reality checks

As the idea for a project takes shape, it's easy to get consumed by anticipation that at last something is being done to solve a problem that's been causing headaches for weeks or months or even years. We naturally want to jump in to solve the problem.

Wise project managers, however, do an initial reality check by addressing two key questions. Is the problem worth solving? Does a feasible solution exist? It's impossible to get definitive answers to those questions at first. But putting in enough effort to make reasonable guesses can help your company avoid wasting time on projects that customers don't care about or for which there's currently no workable solution, or there are solutions that will be too costly to implement.

It is also crucial that you carry that questioning mentality throughout the project, pausing periodically for additional reality checks. How often will depend on the nature of your project. Your project team may go through a rapid learning curve where you uncover surprising facts about the project, the nature of the work involved, customer needs, changing market conditions, etc. In such cases, you may need to do a reality check with management every few weeks.

Performing three checks in addition to the questions raised above can help you know when and if a project charter needs to change:

Check when the problem definition is clearer: This reality check should occur as soon as the team has flushed out the challenges, opportunities, costs, and benefits in more detail. Present the data to management to get approval to proceed as originally planned or modify the project goals accordingly.

Check after a specific solution is identified: This check should focus largely on feasibility. Is the solution idea workable? Affordable? Practical within the time frame needed? Use market studies, pilot testing, prototyping, and/or simulations to help answer those questions.

Check before full-scale implementation: By this point, you should have a good handle on the costs of implementation and risks of not acting. Give management an opportunity to review that information and discuss timing and plans to mitigate risks.

"If the results of a well-conceived and executed feasibility study indicate that the project should proceed, you can move confidently into the planning and implementation phases. If the results are discouraging, . . . use the data to redesign the project and do another feasibility study, and so on, until you've identified a concept that works."

□ ~~Finish what~~ you start

☑ Terminate unworthy projects

The most fundamental objective of a project is to achieve business results. That means providing a certain amount of return on the proposed investment. Yet in too many organizations, management gets complacent, allowing approved projects to proceed without any further assessment of likely payback. As a result, projects that are no longer profitable are allowed to continue on to completion.

This approach is foolhardy, since so many things can change during a project. For example, maybe your team discovers that it will take twice the time or double the costs to achieve the targeted benefits. Or perhaps the solution will affect only a portion of the customer segments. Or customer needs may shift. Or you may stumble onto an even greater opportunity.

In any of these cases, surely your company would be better off in the long run if you revisited the business plan for the project. And that means a *complete* reassessment: looking at *all* investments (time, money, personnel, equipment, materials, etc.) and *all* benefits (customer satisfaction, increased market penetration, bigger revenues, reduced waste, less overhead, etc.). Such a reevaluation should occur at each main stage of the project: after initial exploration, after data collection, after you've identified solutions, and prior to full-scale implementation.

To maximize your company's return on its project investments:

Stay alert to significant changes: It's a mistake to assume that the project estimate at the beginning will stay the same to the very end. Situations change, sometimes quickly, so it's not only possible but likely that conditions will change to alter your original assessment of the business case for a given project. Periodically reevaluate the economic viability of every project.

Avoid the term "failure": In too many organizations, early termination of a project is viewed as failure. To the contrary, stopping a project for the right reasons is smart management: it allows management to divert resources to higher-priority efforts.

Beware of letting inertia win: Every project generates a certain amount of inertia. People develop ownership and the team and its sponsors think, "We really have to see this through to the end." Couple those feelings with the sweat equity invested and you have conditions that favor continuing projects that should be stopped.

"Projects are investments that your company makes, from which they expect a return. . . . Investments can sometimes go bad. In many cases a project should be terminated, though in far too many cases it isn't."

☑ Develop a logical plan

It's odd how some project managers seem to shy away from one of their primary responsibilities: actively managing how the project work gets done. It is this active management that will keep your project on track and let you deliver results on time and within budget.

The cornerstone of active management is having a plan that spells out what you expect to happen. Having the plan documented is essential. That way it can become both a communication tool and a learning tool. Amid the bustle of teamwork, it's easy to forget exactly what commitments were made and by whom. With a written plan, you'll know what resources are needed when. Team members can manage their work themselves because they'll know specifically what work is expected of them. A written document also allows you to compare the plan against reality, so you can adjust accordingly and also educate yourself, so future plans will be more realistic.

For short projects that involve only a few people, the written plan can be simple, perhaps a Gantt chart that depicts major activities spread out over a timeline, with some indication of who is involved in and/or responsible for the actions. Larger projects will require much more sophisticated planning tools, often the use of schedule software that can be instantly updated as tasks are completed, resources change, or new information causes shifts to the plan.

A project plan will be most useful if you:

Start with a network diagram: Identify the project tasks and their relationship to each other—not just sequence (what needs to come first, second, etc.) but also dependencies (which tasks cannot start until another has been completed).

Develop a project control plan: Estimate the durations of all the tasks in the network diagram. After assessing the dependencies, overlay the results onto a timeline that gives specific start and stop dates for each activity. This is your project control schedule.

Identify the critical path: If available, use project planning software to help you identify the linked series of steps that have the least amount of flexibility, that must occur within the scheduled timeframes in order for the project to be done on time.

"The principal output of this portion of the planning process is a control schedule—an activity-based timeline that the team will use as a map for executing the work and that you'll use as a guide for verifying that work is getting done on time."

☑ Leave room for learning

There is a fundamental gap between the level of certainty desired by management and the inherent uncertainty of projects. On the one hand, management wants to make good decisions about how to invest precious resources. On the other hand, the reason for launching a project is to address a need or a problem that your company currently does not know how to address.

So how can you provide certainty without committing yourself to goals, targets, budgets, etc., that turn out to be unworkable once you know more? Walking this line can be one of the trickiest points in any project.

Part of the solution lies in developing a "phase" mentality, where your plans and estimates are divided according to the project phases and the level of uncertainty increases the further out you go.

At the beginning, for instance, you can be reasonably certain about what investment (time, money) is needed to bring the team together, hold your first meetings, and do the initial exploration. Since you don't know what that exploration will reveal, you can't be as certain about what it will take to develop solutions and can have no certainty at all about the costs of those solutions. Once you've completed the initial exploration, you'll have a much better idea of what kinds of solutions you need to investigate and the resources needed to do that investigation.

To navigate your way through the initial uncertainty but avoid looking incompetent:

Match plan details to uncertainty levels: Keep the first drafts of your schedule and budget simple and not very detailed. Divide the timing and budget by phases of the project. The same is true for any graphics. Avoid plans or graphics that indicate a higher level of knowledge than you possess at the moment.

Provide ranges: The more uncertain you are, the wider the range of your estimates will be. The more you learn, the more precisely you can project into the future and the more you can narrow your estimates.

Schedule "phase approval" meetings: Work with management to decide when they want to review the project. Make sure they are clear that each approval pertains only to the completion of the next phase. So, approval for the first phase may mean, "Investigate this issue, then come back to us." A second-phase approval may mean, "Work on these kinds of solutions, then come back to us."

"The level of detail in all your documents should reflect your level of knowledge and certainty."

☐ ~~Manage individually~~

☑ Understand team dynamics

When a team forms, people are more likely to think as individuals, asking themselves questions like, "What's in it for *me*?" (WIIFM) and "What will be expected of *me*?" Over time, they start to identify more as team members: "How will *we* get this work done?"

Helping people make the transition from individuals to team members is part of your responsibility as a project leader. You can't ignore either side of the equation. Helping people get clear about individual expectations reduces anxiety and opens the door for them to begin thinking more like team members. Yet even as they begin doing so, you want people to feel comfortable contributing their ideas and opinions.

The best teams are those that find a balance point at which the members are committed to using their individual talents and skills in support of the team's work. Finding this balance point is not always easy. You can't let individual personalities dominate to the point where the team can't make any progress, but you don't want a team of automatons who've shut off their brains. It will take your skills as a leader and facilitator to help the team develop as a unit.

Avoid wasting time on frivolous team-building activities that bear no relation to the work. Instead, weave group activities into early team meetings to generate something of value, such as brainstorming sessions about customers and their needs or a process observation exercise.

Provide a bridge from individual to team member to build and strengthen bonds:

Address role questions in a team meeting: At one of the first team meetings, review project objectives and explain how the results will benefit the company, its customers, and participants' work areas. Clarify which team members will fill which roles.

Meet with team members individually: Explain to each person why he or she was chosen for the project and what you hope each will contribute. Discuss problems or constraints they may encounter.

Keep individual differences visible: Wanting a team to work well as a unit does not mean discouraging disagreement or differences of opinion. In fact, it means the exact opposite. Make sure that individuals feel comfortable expressing their viewpoints or they will never completely feel like team members.

"Team building is more than a pizza party. . . . The strong forms of team building occur when team members expand their knowledge of each other and the project at the same time."

Introduce processes
as needed

☑ Develop a
configuration plan

Some lucky project managers work for companies that have well-defined standards and procedures for conducting project work. But most of us work at places with minimal documentation or, worse, no formal procedures at all.

Whether you're one of the lucky project managers who will have a good foundation or one of the people who may be starting from scratch, you need to prepare specific guidelines for every project you manage. Think of them as a configuration plan, a description of how you will conduct business on that project.

The basic elements of a configuration plan are what you would expect: a description of who should be involved in the planning, the approach to scheduling, methods for preparing estimates (costs, time, and resources), a list of planning documents and their purpose, and a description of how and how often you will track progress. You should include your communication plan: the stakeholders who need to be kept in the loop and the timing and method for contacting them.

One thing that separates effective project managers from relatively ineffective ones is how much thought they put into documentation and communication from the very beginning of their project.

There's a lot of documentation you could develop. But avoid excess—do only what makes sense and adds value. Documentation, like communication, is exceedingly difficult to do well until you have some experience. Make sure you check for procedures in your company that are already documented. Share these procedures within your team.

To make developing your configuration planning manageable, divide the work into three parts:

Plan the approach: What general approach is best for your organization? (Cross-reference any existing procedures.) What is the best way to define scope? Estimate the effort, duration, and costs. Does your company use graphical summaries of timelines?

Plan the execution and control: How will you measure and verify progress? What constitutes a "change" that needs to be reported? What approvals are required? What guidelines for team meetings and team collaboration do you want to establish and follow?

Plan for communication and personnel needs: What method is preferred for documenting roles and responsibilities? What venues should be used to develop mutual expectations among you, the team, and management? What process do you need to follow to secure staff time for the project? How can you make adjustments?

"Admittedly, it can require substantial effort, but if done properly, documentation can be much more of a friend than a foe."

☑ Manage all project stakeholders

One of the most important things you can do as a project manager is recognize that interfaces are a big part of project life. Your project does not exist in a vacuum. You, your fellow team members, and the work you're doing all have many links to the rest of the organization. The outcome from your project must be woven into the fabric of the organization if you want it to live on long after the project is over.

Learning to recognize and deal with interfaces can have a profound effect on your project—on your level of heartburn during the project and your satisfaction with results months afterwards. From a practical viewpoint, the interfaces you need to care about most are *people*—or, in project management lingo, *stakeholders*.

What makes people stakeholders? Perhaps they stand to gain or lose something with the success (or failure) of the project. They may control resources (money, people, equipment, time) that you need to accomplish the project. Perhaps they will be affected by or use the project outputs. Or they may be accountable for the results to others in your company's management structure. Working well with stakeholders can make your project flow more smoothly. Ignoring them can almost guarantee failure.

Improve the odds of success by actively managing stakeholder relationships:

Get to know your stakeholders: Identify every group or individual that can influence or could be affected by the project. Consider people both inside and outside the company. Meet with them individually (if feasible) to find out what they expect from you and discover their priorities.

Understand your power and influence over them: Whether formal (positional authority) or informal (implied authority), you will have at least some control over some stakeholders simply by virtue of being the project leader. You will likely be able to influence those you can't control.

Develop strategies for dealing with each stakeholder: Not all stakeholders are created equal. Combine your knowledge of stakeholders and their power with your knowledge of your own needs and power to develop appropriate tactics for communicating with and/or directly involving stakeholders.

"It's ordinarily not wise to use positional authority very often, as this can frequently lead to feelings of resentment. . . . People are more likely to respond if you develop your expert power, the ability to gain support through superior knowledge or capability."

☐ Adjust targets as needed

☑ Measure against a baseline

If you don't know where you are now, set no goals, and don't keep track of where you go in the future, it's pretty easy to claim that anywhere you arrive is your destination. Unfortunately, business doesn't work that way. Projects are launched for the purpose of reaching specific business goals. You won't be able to conclusively demonstrate that you've achieved those goals unless you show where the company was when the project started and where it was when it ended.

Providing this proof starts by putting a stake in the ground early in the project—documenting the planned schedules, costs, and desired outcomes, such as design or performance specifications (quality, price, speed, features, etc.). You then need to document reality: When did an action start? End? What were the actual costs? What are the improved performance levels?

The final step is comparing the plans with the reality. You won't hit your estimates dead-on. Nobody does. You'll need to distinguish *performance* problems from *estimation* errors: If performance is below expectations, for example, it could be that your estimates were unrealistic or that the solutions you chose were inadequate. Obviously, deciding on a correct course of action depends on the underlying reason for the shortfall. The same is true if you exceed expectations. Were you too conservative in the estimates? Are you sure you're measuring end performance correctly?

Part of your role as project manager is to guide your team in developing methods for dealing with project information:

Discuss what information is essential: It's easy to get overwhelmed with information. Focus on the information that will be most useful for your decisions about the timing, purpose, and progress of the project.

Identify where the information is generated: If a project got behind or ahead of schedule, who would be the first to know? If customers were unhappy, who would they tell? Will the information just come to you or do you have to go out and seek it?

Decide how to capture the information: Once you know what you want to capture and where the information is generated, decide how and who will capture that information. Develop forms (hard copy or online) that people will find easy to use.

"It's not enough to simply gather information. . . . Information should be in the appropriate form, timely, precise, and credible."

☑ Be objective about threats

Risk and uncertainty are unavoidable in project life. While on the one hand a good project manager has to convey optimism and a positive attitude about accomplishing what needs to be done, it's dangerous to ignore or deny true threats.

Every project faces a range of risks, from the very small (going over budget by $100) to the very large (missing a product release date by six months). Be aware that responding to risks consumes resources. As a savvy project manager, you have to evaluate the threats facing your project, determine which of them are most important to address, and then decide on a course of action.

There are four basic ways to deal with risk. You can avoid the threat: choose a course of action that eliminates exposure. You can transfer the impact of the risk: as with insurance, you don't avoid the risk, but instead make yourself relatively immune to the worst consequences. You can assume the risk: simply proceed with the knowledge that you agree to deal with the consequences if the worst happens. You can prevent or mitigate the risk: take action to eliminate the root cause of the risk or at least lessen its impact.

As we all know, prevention is often the least costly and most reliable strategy for dealing with risk—particularly in situations where the impact is high. Whenever it makes sense, focus on measures that prevent or avoid risks.

Dealing with risk is mostly a matter of planning:

Identify the greatest risks: What parts of the project do you (and your company) know the least about? Consider everything from scope, timing, and cost to technology, resources, and market factors.

Quantify and analyze the risks: Though it can be difficult to do, try to quantify the nature of the risks (such as lost sales if a market window is missed, lower sales if cost targets aren't met, etc.). Determine probability and impact for each risk: the likelihood of the undesired event actually happening and the effect that it would have on the project.

Define a contingency plan: Identify specific courses of action to be taken if a problem occurs. Determine the best approaches for addressing risks that are most likely to occur and/or that would have a severe impact on the project (and customers).

"If you attempt to lead a project without addressing risk and uncertainty . . . you'll continue to bump into things that will throw you in an unplanned direction."

☑ Actively manage communication channels

Communication seems like it should be easy. After all, we do it all the time—chatting with coworkers when we arrive at work in the morning, sending e-mails all day long, calling suppliers or customers. But doing communication well in a business setting is harder than it looks. You not only need to be clear about the messages you want to send; the *way* you communicate is likely to influence other people's impressions of you as much as any other single thing you do.

The options are endless. You need to consider whether the message you want to send will be better received if written (memos, e-mails, reports, updates to communal records) or delivered verbally (face-to-face meeting, phone call). Should you meet with people one on one or in a group setting? Put in a lot of prep time or be impromptu?

A lazy project manager spends little time thinking about these issues and tends to load up team meetings with a lot of "for your information" announcements. Team meeting time is far too precious to waste in communication that could be shared by other means.

To be an effective project manager, you need to put as much thought into planning communication as anything else you do for the team:

Consider the purpose: Are you trying to involve others in a discussion or decision or simply passing along information about a decision or action already taken? Is the information targeted at one person only or many people—and what will they do with the information? What is the long-term goal? You don't want to exclude someone from a meeting who should be involved in a critical decision.

Be efficient: We have all been subject to phone calls, e-mails, and presentations that took far too long to come to the point. Structure the communication to get to the purpose quickly. Follow guidelines for good written or verbal communication so people don't get distracted by unimportant details.

Follow up: Despite our best efforts to be effective communicators, we can't really control *what* other people hear. Get in the habit of following up with people. That way you can check their understanding and clarify any confusion.

"According to some estimates, you can expect to spend more than 80% of your time communicating in some way. You'd better know how to do it well!"

☐ Optimize functional
excellence

☑ Optimize project excellence

Most organizations consist of many functional departments, which can foster a *silo mentality*: People tend to think first of the needs, interests, and goals of their individual departments before considering those of the organization as a whole. This attitude is often destructive in a team setting because what's best for one department may not be best for the project, the company, or its customers.

Your challenge will be redirecting team members' frame of reference from a *functional* orientation to a *project* orientation. A number of forces will be working against you. For one thing, team members often have their own agendas, even in the most benign sense. A marketing person naturally sees the world in terms of customer segments, market trends, etc. An engineer sees the world in terms of practicality and functional specifications. You must learn to recognize these biases and shift them toward a more team-focused attitude.

Also, projects are, by definition, temporary. Where will team members go after the project? Back to their functional responsibilities. And don't overlook the fact that you're not the person who signs their paychecks.

Making the shift from functional to project thinking is easier if you continually reinforce the message that serving the company and its customers is best for individuals in the long run:

Be specific about criteria: When people agree on how a choice or decision will be made, it's easier for them to set aside their personal biases. For example, if everyone agrees that "must improve customer satisfaction" is the most important solution criterion, then no one can object to a solution that does so even if it is not ideal from their perspective.

Use data to make decisions: Require data for all major decisions on the team. If you have criteria and data, it becomes very difficult for people to support personal preferences that aren't best for the project or the company.

Reinforce process thinking: Try to frame issues facing the team in terms of a process. What inputs are needed? Where can you get them? What are the steps? The output? The customers? Even if not directly related to team actions or solutions, it's imperative to encourage process thinking if you want to overcome functional mentalities.

"As a project manager, one of your jobs is to form the team into a unified, single-minded unit with a focused project objective."

☑ Consider post-project issues

Think about projects you've worked on in the past. What was happening six months or a year after the project was officially over? Did the results get preserved? Did someone take ownership and weave them into the way that work is done? Or were your final results captured only in a project binder that then sat on a shelf, collecting dust?

If the results fell into the "collecting dust" category, you're not alone. But you can avoid that fate in the future if everything you plan and do during the project is with a consideration of what will happen after the project is over. This is called *having a full life cycle perspective*. When considering solutions, for example, think about who will have to implement that solution, under *what conditions*, and with *what background and training*. Think about collateral costs in the long term: the ease and cost of maintaining equipment, the ease of updating instructions, and so on.

Your knowledge of how, why, when, and where your project's deliverables will be used should form the basis for making decisions throughout the entire project:

Consider practicality and feasibility: When considering solution ideas, put "practical" high on the list. Having a solution that's slightly less than perfect but that people actually use is much better than a perfect solution that people won't use. The better you understand true customer or user needs, the more likely it is that you will be able to come up with ideals that people *will* use long after the project is over.

Consider long-term ownership: There has to be someone—usually a manager or supervisor in the work area—who will have ownership over the output from your project in the long run. Involve this person in the planning up front. Conduct specific handoff meetings where responsibility is transferred to that person.

Make it easy to do the "new thing": Given the chance, we will all do what is "tried" even if it's no longer so "true." Your project will result in some deliverables that make change necessary—using a new method, offering a new service, following different guidelines. Make sure all workplace instructions, documentation, software, training materials, etc., are updated and use mistake-proofing tactics to make it impossible for people to fall back into old habits.

"What happens after the project is often more important than the project."

☐ ~~Manage everything~~

☑ Manage interfaces

Fledgling project managers often make the mistake of assuming that their primary role is to direct the day-to-day actions of team members. The most benign interpretation is that they simply want to be *informed* about what team members are doing. What's more likely is that they want to *approve and/or advise* on everything that the team members are doing. This approach is guaranteed to enrage experienced team members. It robs team members of confidence in their own skills and judgment.

Micromanaging overlooks another key aspect of team leadership: You're the only person in the organization who has the power to create a healthy working relationship between and among project team members. This is called *interface management*. Without at least some guidance or direction from you, it is unlikely that team members will interact enough. So it is your job to create a framework—procedures, attitudes, principles—that will help team members manage themselves effectively in support of the team.

To equip your team members to use their time wisely:

Make meetings a priority: Most of a team's work happens during meetings because that's where team members share updates on individual assignments, where the team as a whole examines and discusses data, makes decisions, and so on. Having all team members in attendance sets the stage for more effective communication outside of the meeting—which explains why absence from team meetings should be very rare for team members.

Encourage interactions as needed: Set guidelines that make it OK for team members to talk with each other whenever a need arises, rather than waiting for the next team meeting (which could be days or weeks away). Delays waste time—and make it likely team members may miss opportunities for learning as well. Just require that they update you (as project manager) whenever they take important actions or make decisions.

Set team communication guidelines: As a team, talk about when, how, and with whom different kinds of information should be shared. When is it OK to interrupt another team member? When should you as project manager be involved? When does the whole team need to be alerted about new information? What format should people use—in person or through e-mail, voicemail, reports, alerts posted on a bulletin board, etc.?

"Your role in fostering teamwork and synergism may require you to devote some energy to 'designing and engineering' the interaction among team members."

☐ Manage "outwardly"

☑ Practice self-management

With so much to do during a project, it's easy for a project manager to focus solely on managing *other* people—making sure that team members are clear on responsibilities, have the resources to complete tasks, and so on. The most effective project managers, however, have a keen sense of how strong their influence over others really is—even if they have no formal authority—and they learn how to manage and improve their own management skills.

When you think about the players who surround you while on a project, it soon becomes clear why you can't simply wait for feedback to come to you.

Team members will seldom *openly and voluntarily* criticize or comment on a project leader who controls their destiny (at least to some extent). Of course, if they don't like what you're doing, they may make comments behind your back, but that will just undermine your efforts to establish an effective team.

Customers experience only the *outcome* of your work, not the *process*. So they are not in a position to offer helpful insights about how to do your work better.

Similarly, your direct managers aren't directly involved with the day-to-day operations of the team. They may observe more of the process than customers and may occasionally offer tips, but they are typically unpredictable sources of feedback.

To improve your leadership skills:

Become more introspective: After meetings or one-on-one encounters with team members, reflect on the interaction. Did you achieve your goals? Communicate effectively? Did team members leave feelings more positive, more encouraged—or less so? What could you have done differently to handle the situation better? Look for personal biases that are influencing your behavior.

Learn to deal with feedback: The surest ways to guarantee that you never get honest feedback are to ignore other people's opinions or snap their heads off when they try to tell you how they feel about what you did. Creating an environment where people feel free to provide negative feedback and learning how to truly hear it takes practice.

Find a mentor: If you're fortunate enough to work with someone you trust implicitly, whose opinion you value, who will give you honest feedback, and who can observe you on the job, enlist his or her help.

"Some project managers make the mistake of believing that simply because they're constantly surrounded by others they'll receive continuous feedback. . . . This is simply not true."

☑ Recognize multiple success metrics

Every organization has its own view of what matters in project outcomes. You could, of course, just hit a few basic targets, but since the project's success will influence how you will be perceived as a project manager, it pays to take a broader view of project success.

The first level is *meeting expectations*. Note that regular variations on either side—exceeding or falling short of targets—are suspect. Always going above targets means someone is being too conservative; your company may lose opportunities for major breakthroughs. Always falling short means that whoever sets targets has turned a blind eye to your company's true capacity or that you lack the skills to bring the project in on time and within budget. Both situations create unpredictability for the organization.

A second level of success is *project efficiency*. If the project met targets but your customers, team members, or others were adversely affected, it's unlikely to be viewed as successful. Explore multiple ways to evaluate efficiency. How could you measure the level of disruption to your or the client's workplace? What would efficient application of resources look like? What would indicate that your team came through conflict as a stronger unit?

A third level is *customer or user utility*. Was the original problem solved? Was there a verifiable increase in sales, income, or profit? Did you realize the estimated savings? Is the customer (internal or external) actually using the output?

A fourth level is *organizational performance*. What lessons did you learn from the project? How and where are those lessons being applied elsewhere?

To improve the odds of succeeding at all these levels:

Clarify all expectations: Talk to your manager, other project leader, and anyone else to investigate the expectations beyond the obvious (likely pertaining to participation, communication, unofficial boundaries, etc.)

Understand the true need: Push beneath the stated goals to discover the need underlying the project. What is the problem that people are trying to solve, not just the solution they think will work? What is the opportunity?

Document goals and achievements: No one else in the company will be as familiar with the process and outcomes of a project as you and your teammates. Become your own publicity department by documenting success metrics on all four levels.

"High-performing organizations learn from their failures—and their successes—and use that knowledge to improve their success rate over time."

☐ ~~Avoid documentation~~

☑ Use documentation wisely

The last thing that most project managers need is to get swamped in paperwork. But without at least some documentation, a project is more likely to go astray.

Needs for documentation shift over the course of a project. At the beginning, during initiation, you need documents that lay out the purpose, boundaries, and requirements for the project. As you develop a deeper understanding of the desired outcomes, the focus is on plans. How do you expect the project to unfold? What kinds of resources (people, dollars, equipment, etc.) do you need to complete that work?

Once the project is under way, documentation needs to follow two paths. The first is tracking progress against the plan, in part so you can periodically update management. The second is tracking decisions make about the project content: What did you learn about the problem or opportunity? What did you decide to do about it? How did you decide? What solutions resulted? How do you know they will work?

These two paths continue even as the project winds down. First, you need to document the *process* of running the project and lessons learned, both for your own education and to share with others. Second, you need to provide any documentation needed to operate/maintain the changes that resulted from the project.

Above all, as a project manager, you are more than just the leader of a team. You are also the business manager for that portion of your company's operations. Your documentation should reflect that dual reality:

Think like a functional manager: Think about the types of documentation that your manager must ensure are maintained on a regular basis—employee records, contracts, purchase orders, budgets, actual cost, etc. You will need similar documentation for your project.

Distinguish short-term needs from long-term needs: Some documentation is really used only during the project, such as team meeting notes, preliminary data charts etc. Other documentation is intended to live on long after the project ends, such as process maps, instructions for using new procedures, revised purchase codes, or whatever. The former can be kept in any format that suits you best. For the latter, you need to think about the users' needs.

Follow company standards: Some good news is that you don't have to start from scratch. Most companies have documentation on past projects that you can use as a model.

"Proper documentation is a crucial support function of project management. Because each project is unique, no specific level of detail is appropriate for all projects."

☐ Reward heroes

☑️ Reward excellent term behaviors

Probably no area of project management generates as much controversy as how to best reward performance. The subject is a little simpler for project managers than for business managers because they rarely have power over compensation or, at the other end, punishments strong enough to have any lasting effect.

But there are still a lot of dangers to avoid. You can't just do *nothing* about rewards or recognition for teamwork. Imagine how you'd feel if you put a lot of energy into a project and never got any kudos or thanks. But you don't want to make a big deal out of everything or your praise or reward will lose its impact. (Don't give a gold star just because someone shows up at a team meeting!)

You can't consistently recognize the same individuals or the rest of the team members may get discouraged. But if you never recognize superior achievement, the high performers will wonder why they work so hard.

It seems impossible to find the right balance, doesn't it?

To navigate around these problems, the most important criterion a project manager can apply when evaluating potential rewards is asking whether it is more likely to *promote* or to *discourage* teamwork. When you look at it through that lens, you will likely:

Discourage individual heroics: When organizations develop a reputation for rewarding the individual hero who rides in and saves the day, what they get are a bunch of white knights all going off in their own direction. That's the exact opposite of what you need if your goal is to create a high-performing team.

Reward the team as a unit: Yes, you may run a slight risk of offending some "top performers." But overall you'll gain more than you'll lose if you think about ways to acknowledge the team as a whole. And you don't need to get fancy. Pizza lunches, T-shirts with a team logo, thank-you notes from customers. . . . Simple ideas like these do a good job of promoting a positive team attitude.

Involve the team: There's no rule that says rewards must come only from the project leader.

Have your team members develop ideas for ways they can individually or collectively recognize the contributions of fellow teammates or anyone who supports the team.

"Rewards and recognition is one of the most difficult aspects of a project manager's job. . . . I'd urge you to consider . . . that your projects are more likely to succeed when your team members work together to progress as a team."

☑ Maximize learning from closure

You and your fellow team members have worked hard, likely for months on end. As the project comes to a close, there's a loss or energy but yet a reluctance to disband—if the project has been a good experience! Team members may feel irritable about what may be perceived as the "administrivia" required to complete all documentation, get approvals, and so on. The team may start to disintegrate as a functional unit—team members who have completed their tasks may stop attending meetings. Communication may become difficult.

On top of all those team issues, there are the managerial loose ends that you need to take care of personally, such as making sure official records have the final figures, submitting final invoices (and ensuring bills are paid), and closing out accounting codes (if applicable).

Even if your energy level is low, you can't afford to let the project simply drift to an end. Doing so puts the results in jeopardy and may leave people with a sour taste in their mouths.

To close a project successfully, think about acting in the following ways:

Complete the project work: It is your responsibility to ensure that the output from your project (the new product, service, policy, or process) is being used as designed and delivering on the business targets. Since the project output is something that will live on after the project, you need to make sure that *someone*—you or a person in the functional area—has responsibility for following up on all unresolved issues or new problems that arise.

Ease team member transitions: Your visibility should be greater than at any time since the beginning of the project. You need to be super-organized, keep up-to-date lists of final "to-do's," and remind team members of their responsibility in helping to close out those items. Make sure that team members feel a sense of closure, that they don't just drift away wondering what the final outcome was.

Coordinate customer relationships: Your project has a customer or customers—the people who are going to use or benefit from the project. Being somewhat formal in having the customers accept the results is a good way to not only maintain strong customer relationships but also acknowledge the team's accomplishments.

"The close-out phase of the project should be given as much or more project management attention as any other phase of the project. Bringing a project to a successful conclusion requires close attention."

☐ Move on when finished

☑ Transfer your "lessons learned"

Organizations that are on the rapid road of improvement learn how to mine every experience for the benefit of the organization as a whole. One of the best ways to spread the benefits of your project beyond the project boundaries and support continuous improvement in project management in your organization is in the form of a lessons-learned study. Performing a systematic review of project experiences will help you understand the nature of both the positive and the negative experiences—lessons that you can then pass on to other project managers in your company.

The first part of a lessons-learned study is for your team to review documentation about problems related to project management that you captured throughout your project. If such notes were not kept, review meeting agendas and records to see if they spark any memories.

The second part is expanding your knowledge base by performing a 360° review, getting input from all stakeholders (including team members, support personnel, customers, management, and staff in affected work areas). This review can take many forms, but is often modeled after a brainstorming session in a team meeting: that is, you bring people together, present them with a clear objective, brainstorm to elicit ideas, then sort and organize the results.

Probably the most valuable output from a lessons-learned study will be information you can share about problems encountered and ways to avoid them in the future. Be general in your thinking: obviously, no one is going to conduct a project exactly like yours, but surely there are or will be other projects addressing similar issues or structured very similarly to yours.

Finally, don't just generate a list of "what went well" and "what didn't go well." That won't help anyone apply what you learned. Instead, you should do the following:

Document problems and their impact: What problems do your stakeholders recall? What was the impact on them?

Explore root causes: What's your best guess as to why a particular problem occurred? What can you do to verify that cause? Why wasn't the problem anticipated beforehand? (Look for problems in planning, monitoring, and control.)

Capture suggested improvements: How can future teams avoid the problem? If it can't be entirely eliminated, how can it be detected sooner? What actions would help lessen the impact? Is there a centralized database where you can document your ideas? If not, can you help create one?

"If you do not structure your information so that others can actually apply the lesson you've learned, your organization hasn't really benefited."

"One of the biggest shifts in behavior (and thinking) you'll encounter will be the need to rely upon others to get things done. . . . You'll quickly discover that there's far too much for you to do alone, yet delegation will prove to be a challenge. Empowering others, and then trusting them to follow through, may be unsettling."

"Project management is both an art and science. The art is strongly tied to the interpersonal aspects—the business of leading people. The science identifies and explains the processes, tools, and techniques."

The McGraw-Hill Mighty Manager's Handbooks

The Powell Principles
by Oren Harari (0-07-144490-4)

Details two dozen mission- and people-based leadership skills that have guided Colin Powell through his nearly half-century of service to the United States.

Provides a straight-to-the-point guide that any leader in any arena can follow for unmitigated success.

How Buffett Does It
by James Pardoe (0-07-144912-4)

Expands on 24 primary ideas Warren Buffett has followed from day one.

Reveals Buffett's stubborn adherence to the time-honored fundamentals of value investing.

The Lombardi Rules
by Vince Lombardi, Jr. (0-07-144489-0)

Presents more than two dozen of the tenets and guidelines Lombardi used to drive him and those around him to unprecedented levels of success.

Packed with proven insights and techniques that are especially valuable in today's turbulent business world.

The Welch Way

by Jeffrey A. Krames (0-07-142953-0)

Draws on the career of Jack Welch to explain how workers can follow his proven model.

Shows how to reach new heights in today's wide-open, idea-driven workplace.

The Ghosn Factor

by Miguel Rivas-Micoud (0-07-148595-3)

Examines the life, works, and words of Carlos Ghosn, CEO of *Nissan* and *Renault*.

Provides 24 succinct lessons that managers can immediately apply.

How to Motivate Every Employee

by Anne Bruce (0-07-146330-5)

Provides strategies for infusing your employees with a passion for the work they do.

Packed with techniques, tips, and suggestions that are proven to motivate in all industries and environments.

The New Manager's Handbook

by Morey Stettner (0-07-146332-1)

Gives tips for teaming with your employees to achieve extraordinary goals.

Outlines field-proven techniques to succeed and win the respect of both your employees and your supervisors.

The Sales Success Handbook

by Linda Richardson (0-07-146331-3)

> Shows how to sell customers—not by what you tell them, but by how well you listen to what they have to say.

> Explains how to persuasively position the value you bring to meet the customer's business needs.

How to Plan and Execute Strategy

by Wallace Stettinius, D. Robley Wood, Jr., Jacqueline L. Doyle, and John L. Colley, Jr. (0-07-148437-X)

> Provides 24 practical steps for devising, implementing, and managing market-defining, growth-driving strategies.

> Outlines a field-proven framework that can be followed to strengthen your company's competitive edge.

How to Manage Performance

by Robert Bacal (0-07-148439-8)

> Provides goal-focused, common-sense techniques to stimulate employee productivity in any environment.

> Details how to align employee goals and set performance incentives.

Managing in Times of Change

by Michael D. Maginn (0-07-148436-1)

> Helps you to understand and explain the benefits of change, while flourishing within the new environment.

> Provides straight talk and actionable advice for teams, managers, and individuals.

About the Author

Gary R. Heerkens PMP, PE is a consultant, trainer, lecturer, and author in the field of project management. He is the president of Management Solutions Group, a Rochester, New York based company that specializes in providing project management educational solutions and organizational development support.